A Simple Guide To Voyaging The Energetic Universe

Awaken To The Power Within You
And Live Life Supremely Well

Michael Webster

ISBN: 978-1-291-96031-0 (sc)
ISBN: 978-1-4834-1871-1 (e)

Because of the dynamic nature of the Internet, any web addresses or
links contained in this book may have changed since publication and
may no longer be valid. The views expressed in this work are solely those
of the author and do not necessarily reflect the views of the publisher,
and the publisher hereby disclaims any responsibility for them.

Lulu Publishing Services rev. date: 09/29/2014

DEDICATION

To my lovely Stella.

You demonstrate unconditional love just by being who you are. I do not have the words to fully express my love for you, and the gratitude I feel that you chose me. All I can say is thank you for everything.

To my children; Michael, Lana, Colette, Karen and Mark, in the hope that this book will motivate and inspire you in a way that I was unable to.

CONTENTS

ACKNOWLEDGEMENTS

The foundations for this book were sketched out sixty six years ago when I had my first experience of unity with the Universe. Since that time many people - knowingly or unknowingly - have helped me along my way.

My first formal teacher, a yogi called Helen Mason–Ellis, helped me at the age of 26 to understand my profound experiences of the Energetic Matrix. At that time the teacher was there but the student was not ready. It was only after her death that I really understood what she had tried to teach me.

To Joy and Mary, Ann and Doreen, the Orkney 'Shamanic' group who undertook to train me in the way of energy and spirit. I managed to maintain my position as a slow and stubborn learner. To Stuart Hepburn, NLP Master Practitioner, Trainer and friend who gave me the gift of NLP at a time when I badly needed it. Stuart remains an inspiration, not only to me but to all who know him. To Huang Po for making me laugh and providing clear instructions for the journey along the universal path. To Evelyn, Gary and Des who were the first Waveform students, and to the many who have since contributed and also benefited from the growing development of Waveform; in particular Joe McHugh, Ray Pawlett and Alan Leith. My thanks for your contributions in the past and good luck in your new enterprises.

My thanks to those who had faith in us and brought us to many countries in the world and to our present European team, Nicky, Erici and Wulf. To Jean-Gil who represents us in Canada and France and is already translating the book into French. To my son Michael for bringing the book to other people through his media skills. To our accountant, Chris, who nagged me to write the book. To Martin Armitage-Smith for his thoroughness and sound advice which has made all the difference to the presentation of this book. My thanks to all our students across the globe from whom I learn more and more.

Finally, my deepest thanks to my wife Stella for her faith and unfailing love and support, for proof-reading the manuscript and for pulling this reluctant recluse kicking and screaming out of his cave.

Mike Webster. July 2014 - Loch Lomond, Scotland

FOREWORD

Several years ago I was fortunate to meet Mike and his wife-to-be, Stella, at a Remote Viewing course on Loch Lomond. Remote Viewing is one of those things in life which shouldn't work, but does. With a multi-step protocol developed for the most sceptical of Cold War warriors, anyone can learn it. Waveform, by contrast, is a more immediate, subtle and direct method of attunement to the invisible matrix of energy that is all around us – if only we bothered to notice.

This deceptively slight book holds up a torch to this invisible world. In so doing, it helps the reader connect to the deeper reality of their felt experience and their own full potential as an active participant in the matrix. Waveform also offers the opportunity to re-examine many beliefs or habits of a lifetime, which may no longer serve the reader.

Mike teaches with calmness, authority and lashings of good humour. There is a warmth and groundedness about the courses that he runs with Stella, which attract men and women from many backgrounds.

May your voyage into the matrix be full of joy and surprise.

Martin Armitage-Smith London August 2014

INTRODUCTION

This book contains simple guidelines and advice for those who are ready to voyage into the energy field and explore the amazing potential of human consciousness.

This book is a thin book - a pocket book - as one does not need something the size of 'War and Peace' to provide information about how to first of all recognise and then access the Energetic Matrix. More words and explanation do not necessarily mean more understanding. They may stimulate the intellect but the intellect is one of the biggest stumbling blocks to direct experience of the Energetic Matrix.

In the excellent translation by John Blofeld of 'The Zen teaching of Huang Po on the Transmission of Mind' Huang Po, a 9th Century Chan (Zen) Master, constantly chided those who kept harping on about the importance of certain practices and beliefs within Buddhism, such as the dharma, the ten stages of progress, the four rewards for the virtuous and wise living (the list is almost endless) and their relevance in gaining enlightenment. Huang Po shocked his listeners when he stated that these are but tools to be discarded - even the Buddha!

I bought this book in the late 60s and read it over and over again. I found it stimulating and inspiring but, 25 years later and reading the book for the umpteenth time, I started to laugh. The penny had dropped at last. I realised that the 132 pages of recorded discourse and the essence of Huang Po's message could be summed up in two sentences. I can almost hear him laughing now.

Huang Po's message was simple. For those prepared to listen with an open mind it provided a guideline into accessing the Energetic Matrix and recognising our place in the Universe. Huang Po's message is contained within the pages of this book. The key to understanding is simple and timeless, and is in front of you right now.

1

THE ENERGETIC MATRIX

'A rose by any other name would smell as sweet.'

Ask 100 people what they think the Energetic Matrix is and you will receive 100 different answers. They may each have an element of the truth in what they believe, but not one will have the whole truth. The problem is that when you name or label something there is a danger that you place a limitation on your experience of it and a label or name does not mean the same thing to everyone. We will, however, look in more detail at these influencing factors and how they affect our perception of reality in another chapter.

Science tells us that matter, as we know it, only makes up about 5% of all that exists in the Universe. 95 % of all that is out there in the Universe is yet to be confidently discovered and identified. Scientists only know the 95% that is out there really exists by the effect is has on the bit we do know about.

We know that the Energetic Matrix is there because we can experience its effects on our lives. Once we know how to enter this always present 'other world' we can enter again and again into this dimension where the possibilities are limitless and natural laws and limitations of our ordinary life do not apply.

1

As we expand our levels of awareness and the depth of our experience we begin to realise that, whatever this dimension IS, it is responsive, it is self-aware, it is evolving and it appears to be limitless. It is constantly present within us and around us. We know it is there by the experiences that it creates for us.

Exactly what it IS, however, we do not know.

For the purpose of this book let us just call it 'The Energetic Matrix', draw a big circle around all the names and labels used to describe the EM, accepting everything and move forward from there.

2

PROGRAMMING AND PRECONCEPTIONS

The key to expanding awareness and a new perception of life is not about time served, boxes ticked, tools collected or development of the intellect. It is about 'Readiness' which is the result of letting go of labels and concepts, recognising and challenging our self-limiting programming, being open, and accepting the reality of our direct experience.

Programming and preconceptions are the stumbling blocks to expanding awareness and inhibit growth and development within the Energetic Matrix.

Programming starts at birth as the uncluttered mind of the child is slowly filled with labels and concepts, dos and don'ts, what is and what isn't. This process continues throughout our lives, through school, university, in relationships and work as we try and fit into what is expected of us. Our individual map of the world has taken shape, containing our programmed fears, doubts about ourselves and the world and our preconceptions about how things are, or *should* be.

Our world has become narrow to the point that anything that challenges our map and belief system is regarded with suspicion or is just incorrect! We may even doubt the reality of our own experience if it challenges our map of the world and dearly held beliefs.

A doctor taking part in one of our workshops, on seeing the human energy field for the first time, and in colour said, 'I know what I am seeing but I don't believe it!'

We can spend our lives clinging to our maps of the world, completely oblivious to the magic that is happening all around us.

There is a joke in our family about me being unable to find the butter in the fridge. I open the fridge and completely fail to see the butter that is right in front of me. The reason is that subconsciously I am looking for butter in a silver wrapper – butter in a plain wrapper does not exist and therefore is completely invisible to me. If it is not part of my map and programming it does not exist.

Much of our programming is designed to keep us alive. Without it many of us would not have survived beyond childhood. Some of our programming has, however, moved beyond its 'sell-by date' and no longer serves us in adult life where experience has led us to form our own opinions.

Early programmes from childhood or adolescence, which tell us that we are not good enough or bright enough to do this or that, can, when carried into adulthood, inhibit our potential as human beings. Programmes such as these can be so completely entrenched/ anchored in our being and our belief system about ourselves that we would not dare challenge them. It takes courage to put behind you an entrenched belief that you have carried around with you for 20-30-40 years or more.

'I know what I am seeing but I don't believe it!'

Some students prefer to return to the safety of their old map and belief system. This may include, as I once witnessed a teacher say to a student, 'It will take you at least 15 years to get as good as me energetically, and I will have moved on by then.' Guess how long the student is going to take to be 'as good as' the teacher? A nice piece of programming, which risks binding the student to the teacher for years to come.

Programming leads to preconceptions - this is what I expect; this is how things should be - thereby closing the door to insight and creativity. This is not only true in how we perceive the world but also in how we perceive ourselves. Both outer and inner preconceptions of how everything 'should be' will be addressed in this short book.

The Matrix opens its doors to you when you are 'ready', not as a result of the time you have served or have waited for something to happen, good works or the practices you have carried out - these are man-made. The Energy Field has been around for at least as long as the Universe has been in existence and it is constantly changing on a local and universal level.

The Energy Field has not read the many books written by man about what it does and how it works. It does, however, provide us with the opportunity to learn and expand our awareness of it every second of our lives. We just have to let go of all we know and all we think we know.

When you are open and ready the Matrix will teach you.

3

ACCESSING THE
ENERGETIC MATRIX

'In order to know what is possible it has to be perceived directly.'

To access the Energetic Matrix one has first of all to recognise it is actually there. Your programming from training of one kind or another may tell you that it is like this or like that, blinding you as to what is actually present (remember the butter in the fridge). Our programming is therefore something we have to recognise and challenge each time it arises, clearing a space for new experiences of reality.

Become a conscious 'Receiver'

The next step is to realise that you are constantly transmitting and receiving information, both energetic and emotional. Everyone else is also receiving this information and can access it - that is if they know how to. This information is like a ripple on a lake. From a small starting point it spreads out to cover the whole lake.

Imagine that you are standing up to your waist in a still lake, which stretches in all directions as far as the eye can see. On the horizon the sky and the lake meet seamlessly. If we look around the lake for signs of movement our focus narrows to the small area we are searching. We can completely miss the ripple of movement behind us, or to one side of us.

If we remain in an open 'Receiver' mode, a position of relaxed alertness, we can instantly be aware of a ripple starting from anywhere in the lake and can bring our awareness to that point to gather more information as required. When you wake on hearing a sound in the night, every part of you - all your senses - reaches out to locate the source of the sound. If you carry out the same exercise in a more relaxed way, this is 'Receiver' mode.

The Frame of Reference / Field of Awareness

The act of opening up our senses and awareness in a specific area is called forming a Frame of Reference (FOR). A FOR can be limited to yourself and someone else, to the people in a room, to include buildings around you when walking down a street. What the FOR encompasses is completely up to you.

The FOR can also be an area that you are not included in, such as a room you are about to go into. The FOR is not inhibited by walls or physical boundaries. Setting a Frame of Reference enables us to gather energetic and emotional information within a specific area.

The Matrix is constantly changing, and in order to recognise what is changing within the FOR we establish first of all what the 'Environment' consists of.

The Energetic Environment

A very good example of understanding and recognising the environment took place in our home a few years ago when we were hosts to two Canadian friends, Olga and Jean-Gil.

One morning, looking out through our lounge window, I saw a deer down the field close to the woods. I pointed it out to my guests. After a slight pause Jean-Gil saw the deer, but Olga didn't. I started to explain to Olga exactly where the deer was, using points of reference like a single large oak tree, and a fence which ran down to the wood, and still Olga didn't see the deer which eventually wandered off.

I realised that seeing or not seeing the deer depended on your recognition and understanding of the environment. Jean-Gil was from Rigaud near Montreal, and his home for much of his life was amongst the trees and woods which encircled his house. Olga lived in Ottawa in a modern, urban environment and was surrounded by buildings. Nature was present in the gardens and verges but it played very little part in Olga's life.

Although all the information was available to both of them, only one of them recognised it, and knew what to do with it.

Forming a FOR only takes a fraction of a second; establishing the feel of the environment a second or two at the most.

We are now ready to identify any energetic and emotional changes that take place within the FOR. Once we know what energetic signals and emotional resonances feel like, we will become aware of the strong emotional and energetic signals that attract our attention by overriding our filters and an established FOR.

The Human Energy Field

The Human Energy Field (HEF) exists within us and around us. What is quite apparent to me is that when the HEF is seen directly it is not as depicted in many books as neat coloured layers like those of an onion.

The HEF is seen as ghost-like clouds of different colours which can be observed to change over a period of time. Sometimes two colours seem to occupy the same place as we change the way we observe the field. Most of the changes, expansion and contraction shown by the changing colours can be seen to take place around the head in response to thoughts and feelings. Colours around the body change more slowly than around the head in response to the needs of the body, chemical changes and cycles.

The brightness or otherwise of the field can reflect excitement, physical exertion and wellness (bright), also depression, inactivity and illness (dull). As these clouds of colour expand, contract and transform within the near field, 'structures' of all shapes and sizes can be detected within it.

If you stand near a person and, starting at their head, move your hand side-ways through their field roughly in line with the contours of their body, about 1/3 metre away you will find discrete 'textures' that are quite different to the overall feel of the person's field. Sometimes what can be found can only be described with words such as prickly, vibrating, hot, buzzy etc.

Direct experience of these structures is what this exercise is about; what these structures *are* and what they are doing in the field is of no importance at this time – so leave aside labels and concepts which are the products of the left brain.

Moving further away from the physical body, more structures can be found in the field. These structures are usually much larger and of a variety of shapes.

Moving close to the physical body and scanning with the hand just above the surface of the torso and limbs, we find another set of structures. Some of these structures may quickly disappear as we make direct contact with them; others defy attempts to make them change.

As we are unique individuals it would not come as a surprise to also hear that no two energy fields are alike, so each new experience of the field is absolutely unique. Once again, it is important to remain in the role of an impartial observer with these exercises. You will learn a great deal as you gain more and more direct experience of the field and how it responds to you just being there.

When two people meet, two vibrating energy fields come together and a process of adjustment takes place, each field responding to the other. The result is that during this interaction the process of energetic change and transformation is accelerated and a new FOR is formed.

For therapists and healers this means that the FOR that existed at the beginning of an appointment will not be the same as the FOR at the beginning of a treatment. One cannot therefore rely on any preconceptions about the diagnosis and energetic treatment which arise from the case history or a discussion with the client. For the treatment to be as effective as it can be, the treatment has to be based on what arises from the new FOR which has come into being during the consultation.

As we will discuss in another chapter, the process of change starts from the moment the client contacts the therapist, whether directly, face to face or over the phone. Each individual's energy field can be located at any distance, anywhere.

Many books show these onion skin layers and label them with various levels from the physical body, then the etheric body and so forth to the finest body (i.e. the layer furthest away from the physical body) which is called the causal or divine body. Wonderful colourful diagrams showing these bodies and their layers are very misleading.

A/ When actually seen, the aura or HEF is not in neat layers like an onion skin - quite the opposite in fact.

B/ If we accept that the universal mind/ the spiritual aspect of ourselves was already in evidence - the centre of our being - this means that all layers are superimposed on the spiritual layer in reverse order, as the bodies which are progressively more dense progress towards the formation of the densest of the bodies - the physical human body.

If this is true, it means that all 'layers' can be accessed from anywhere in the human energy field.

4

THE TOOLS OF ENERGETIC RECOGNITION AND CHANGE

The experience is there – a new reality is forming which has always been there but not seen. The tools to access and explore more deeply into the Matrix are there. They are already 'ours' and have always been accessible to us but we may be completely unaware of them.

The key to accessing the tool of 'Receptors' is readiness. The student voyager has now learned to recognise the energetic environment, the human energy field and the structures, clumps of 'stuff', different qualities and textures in and around the Human Energy Field (HEF) within a chosen Frame of Reference (FOR).

The student voyager is now ready to move forward once more.

***Receptors** – A tool for accessing energetic change and the potential for energetic change within the energetic Field.*

With some assistance from the teacher, the student voyager is now 'brought into receptors'. The teacher enables them to access the tangible experience of receptor response, and shows how to access their receptors whenever they wish. This could be described as bringing intuition to a sensory, conscious level which is accessed at will and immediate in its response.

From this moment on the field comes alive and the student starts to intercept transmissions from the Energetic Matrix that they were unaware of before. The student experiences that some of those 'clumps' and 'textures' are responding to them and interacting with them and others are not responding at all. How can this be?

Students quickly realise that if they physically interact with a structure, place their hand in contact with an energetic structure which responds to them, its quality and level of 'busyness' changes quickly. The structure becomes calmer, and our receptors' response is noticeably less than when they first encountered the structure. The student may also notice that those areas that were initially not responsive may now have become active, whilst other areas remain inactive.

For a therapist working with energy this information is invaluable for carrying out effective energy treatments. In life and work, receptor activity can detect energetic changes that precede emotional and mood change, whatever your environment, be it a room, a train, a group of people, with or amongst animals. It can save your skin and maybe your life!

The energetic signal is immediate and not hampered by distance and the signal is also not influenced by time.

During my years of energy training in Orkney I had an insight into the usefulness of a tool I would one day be able to access at will anywhere and at any time.

A friend and I were in the town of Kirkwall on the mainland of Orkney in one of the local waterfront bars. It was one of the first bars that could be accessed by thirsty fishermen after weeks at sea as it was just across the road from the harbour. The bar was not unduly crowded but had its usual intake of fishermen fresh from the sea, still wearing their waders and waterproofs.

We had just sat down with our second pint when suddenly a change took place in the feel of the room. My friend and I looked around the room and then looked at each other. Nothing seemed to be amiss but, without another word, we got up and quickly left the bar, second pint untouched.

We had just stepped out into the street when the first chair hit the wall beside the door we had just left by. A fight of reasonable proportions had broken out.

We had detected the energetic change that preceded the emotional and mood changes, leading to the action that was now taking place.

Although we may deliberately form a FOR to access energetic change within a specific area, we may become aware of strong signals which we realise are coming from outside the FOR. The bar in the Orkney story was within the FOR. However, other signals may come into our awareness because of the strength of the signal or because the source of the transmitting signal is known to us.

A good example of this is the mother who becomes intuitively aware that all is not well with her child who is many miles away. The mother acts without considering whether her concern is rational or not.

In life as in business, receptor response provides valuable information about a situation, whether it is family around the dinner table, or goings on in a shop or in the boardroom. How this tool can be most effectively used requires careful and constructive guidance combined with a great deal of practice.

You have the potential to cross distance and time and access what is beyond.

With Receptors, and your second natural skill of Emotional Resonances, you can create change and obtain emotional information in real time and in the past.

You are almost ready to voyage in the universe.

5

EMOTIONAL RESONANCES –
THE PERSON AND THE
UNIVERSE

For those who are aware and know how to look within,
each of us is an open book.

Our emotional responses to our thoughts and the situations we find ourselves in are being continuously transmitted to the rest of the world. This is not one-way traffic; we are also receiving information others are endlessly transmitting.

Thankfully we have developed 'filters' that limit the amount of information that we are aware of at any time and, without these filters, we would be an 'open all hours' receiver for the energetic and emotional information transmitted, at least throughout this planet of ours, if not the universe.

We also have choice, and can create boundaries and use our filters to allow or limit the amount of information we receive at any time. This enables us to access the Energetic Matrix and voyage from choice, not from conditions that we cannot control but actually control us. We do have, however, the ability to operate within the Energetic Matrix and also return to life within our filters and the normally recognised range of our five senses.

We can also choose to step into the Matrix and access the energetic and emotional information that we consider to be important.

In her book, 'Home to the Wilderness', Sally Carrighar tells the story of a small boy who had an unusual relationship with birds that came very close to him.

A young girl, observing this, tried to copy what the boy did and remain very still. The birds, however, kept away. The girl said to the boy, 'I am staying very quiet and still, and still the birds do not come to me as they do to you, why is this?' The boy replied, 'It is not what you do; it is how you are inside!'

The face that we present to the world is not how we are inside. If we just look at and listen to someone, we do not access the real person. This person may not realise that there is another part of them transmitting information that they may not be aware of.

We may consciously select a face to present to the world. However, our subconscious mind responds to situations and questions far more quickly than the conscious mind.

We also call this relationship between the conscious and the subconscious mind the 'relationship between head and heart'. The response of the subconscious mind to difficult questions and situations is called an Emotional Resonance, which can be intercepted and interpreted before the conscious mind has time to prepare a verbal response. (In another chapter we will discuss the benefits of each of us bringing the conscious mind and the subconscious mind into alignment – so they sing in unison.)

A human lie detector

A friend of mine called me a human lie detector. This is true only in respect of situations where the truth could be embarrassing, harmful, disempowering or damaging to the person being questioned.

The measure of the emotional response is directly proportional to the importance of the question and the consequences of the answer to the person being questioned.

When my son was 15 years old he asked me what I meant by an emotional response. So I asked him, 'When did you have sex last?' As the shock hit, but before he could say anything, I cut in: 'Now THAT is an emotional response - but don't tell me anything!'

I imagine when he reads this now, there will be an equally strong emotional response!

The student voyager is now ready to be shown how to access at will and experience the emotions each person unwittingly transmits - the reality that lies behind the face that we and others present to the world. The opening of this new door into the Energetic Matrix brings with it a deepening of responsibility in how this new skill is applied, and is not to be taken lightly. Ethical considerations and full acceptance of responsibility for the application of their new skills are pre-requisites for the student to be accepted for further training.

A book, no matter how good, will never replace personal tuition. This is one reason why a detailed description of acquiring of receptors and accessing emotional resonances is not included in this book. These skills and exercises are not learned, they are experienced. This direct personal experience is the most important part of the whole process, challenging the individual programming that arises and the preconceptions and expectations as to how things 'should' be. If we were to include detailed descriptions and analysis of some of the exercises and their outcomes we provide in training we would rob the student of the immediacy and reality of his/her own experience that emerges through the training process.

Practical Application

Having shown the student how to access emotional resonances, we now put this new skill immediately to the test.

How much do we know about ourselves?

Creating a list of carefully structured questions, and working with a partner, we and they can find out just how much each are aware of the emotional responses unwittingly being transmitted.

In order to provide the right conditions to receive and note their responses to the questions, there are some important points to bear in mind.

1/ The questions asked are 'closed questions'. The answer is either yes or no!

2/ The questions are of a searching nature about areas of their lives and are produced unexpectedly from a selection of non-invasive questions that can be 'open questions'.

   a) Are you having enough fun in life?

   b) Are your getting the amount of support that you would like in your work/personal life?

   c) Do you enjoy your job?

Is their response to your questions and the information that they transmit in accord or are they communicating conflicting messages?

When you feed back to them their incongruent answers, you will often find that they have no idea that they had transmitted contradictory information. Given time to think and internalise each incongruent answer, they start to discover the truth that lies within the Emotional Resonances which they may not have realised or had deliberately hidden, even from themselves.

When on the 'receiving end' of the questions, how much did you learn about yourself?

How often do you get asked about those important areas of your life such as:

1/ Do you get enough **fun** in life?
2/ Do you feel **support**ed in your life/your work?
3/ Do you have a clear **vision** about what you want/where you are going in life?
4/ Do you have a **plan** about how you are going to get there/move forward in life?
5/ Do you have the discipline and **structure** from which to move forward?

Ask yourself these questions again. Read them aloud to yourself or ask someone to read them for you. Think about how you feel when you hear them and take note of these feelings.

Moving on:-
How would you like life to be?
What are you going to do about making the changes you want in life?
What is your first step?
When will you take this step?
Date ....?
Time ....?
A decision made without a starting date and time for action remains just a dream.
This exercise is your first step towards **Personal Alignment.**

Applying your new skill in the wide world

Our students come from all walks of life - homemakers, doctors, airline pilots, businessmen and women, CEOs of companies, private investigators, therapists of various disciplines, interested people who want to get more out of life. The skills of Receptors and Emotional Resonances (ER) can be usefully applied in all walks of life.

For example we can learn to recognise frequencies denoting anxiety and fear which may be transmitted underneath but simultaneous to an outburst of anger; similarly we might be able to pick up the real meaning behind the words 'I'm fine!'

Anyone can be trained to recognise and interpret body language, subtle signals that provide clues as to the reality of how we think and what we feel. We can also train ourselves to develop new behaviours that cover up or mask the reality of our responses, our feelings and thoughts. Unless someone is a pathological liar, however, the emotional response to a carefully phrased or unexpected question is transmitted and received before any 'cover-up' can be prepared or implemented. Any incongruence between the verbal response and transmitted emotion is noted. The variety of situations where accessing ERs can be usefully applied is unlimited.

In police work an incongruent response to a question can lead to a new line of questioning, or confirm a chosen line of enquiry, based on information already known.

In an interviewing context, is that CV really that good?

Which team members are not 'pulling their weight' in the team?

Have you done your homework?

One of our graduates is blind and works in drug and alcohol rehabilitation. In seeking to establish whether her clients are following their regime or not, selected questions, carefully timed, reveal the truth. Nothing significant remains hidden from her.

In airports not everyone can be stopped and checked for drugs, weapons or bombs in their luggage or on their person. Combined with their other trained skills and abilities, airport police, scanning for emotional unease as people pass with their luggage, may be able to more easily discount those that are naturally nervous when passing through customs (as many are) from those that have genuine reason to be nervous.

One of our graduates ('L') works with children with special needs. L's ability to detect a change in emotions in a room, crowded with children of different ages, sizes and needs, has proved to be invaluable for the safety of other children and the teachers.

In one instance L picked up a change in a room, her FOR, and in particular, a malevolent transmission which came from one of the larger children who had an aggressive track record towards not only children but also teachers. L realised that this child was slowly and purposely making his way across the room towards one of the teachers. His intention had been transmitted ahead of him and L intercepted him before he reached the teacher, and invited him to come into the garden with her. Taken by surprise by L, the child's manner changed and he quietly went out into the garden with L. The tension in the room, the FOR, eased.

As shown in the illustration of the mother and child, Emotional Resonances as well as Receptor Responses travel any distance. The source of either signal can be located and any person can check their loved ones for signs of stress anywhere, over any distance.

The transmission of emotions can reveal the presence of someone who cannot be seen. A private investigator, who we know, saved himself from serious assault after ERs revealed 3 persons lying in wait for him as he arrived to interview a suspect.

Remember, when a transmission is made, everyone gets the 'message' but not everyone recognises that they have received it. If you are open, and ready to receive transmissions, you will gain subliminal knowledge and information as required. In other situations you are forewarned of things to come and can take beneficial pre-emptive action.

As this book is about the expansion and development of self through greater awareness of the energy field, as well as external application of energetic tools, we will be looking at how ERs connect us to the Universal Mind, and what we can learn from this to bring ourselves more in tune with ourselves and the Universe.

6

BEING PRESENT AND AWARE

To see the world in a grain of sand
And heaven in a wild flower
Hold infinity in the palm of your hand
And eternity in an hour.

Our conscious mind is like a grasshopper, jumping from one thing to another. In the space of a few seconds our conscious mind will happily leap from the present to the past, to the future and back to the present.

When we access the Energetic Matrix we enter a dimension that is intelligent and self-aware. The Matrix is in a constant state of change and you are a guest welcomed to observe and participate in each moment that will never be the same again. Full participation in your invited role in the Matrix can only be carried out in a frame of mind that is fully present and aware.

There is no space for your programming or your personal map of the world. There is no space for intellectualisation, logic or rational thinking. There is no place for labels or concepts, there is only this place which IS.

If we remove the labels we place on everything, also our concepts and judgements AND perceive without analysis, we will see life as it truly is.

If we let go of the tools and take a leap of faith we create an opportunity and space to directly experience a new perception of life. William Blake's words at the beginning of this chapter sum it up beautifully.

One school of thought is that the key functions of the two lobes of the brain and the workings of the mind are as follows:

The left hemisphere contains the conscious, rational mind that analyses, labels and judges with thoughts that alternate between the past and the future. It is concerned with deliberate focus on a narrow frame of reference.

The right hemisphere is the intuitive and creative part of the brain from which insights arise. Its focus is broad and wide-ranging.

It would appear that when the left (analytical) brain is active, the right (creativity and insight) brain is reduced in its ability to be creative.

It was also noticed that when insight/creativity did occur the rational brain was silent, and the visual cortex at the back of the head reduced sight to a defocused state. This may account for part of the reason why many of our greatest innovators (right brain dominant) did not do well at school. People like Bill Gates (Microsoft) Richard Branson (Virgin) Thomas Edison (Inventor).

The claims of many sages over the centuries, Including those of Krishnamurti and Huang Po, are that only when the rational mind is stilled when the rational analytical mind is stilled can creativity occur and insight arise to a conscious level where it can be recognised, would now appear to be confirmed.

Several years ago I took a small party of students to a favourite wood where there were waterfalls, bluebells and many things in nature to delight the eyes and the ears. We walked in single line down the narrow path between trees in glorious green, bluebells and ferns that rested beside the chuckling stream.

I observed that two students behind were constantly talking and apparently unaware of the beauty that was all around them. I was so taken with the sounds, sights and smells I didn't notice what they were saying to each other. My friend Jean-Gil started to laugh, so I listened to the conversation going on behind us. The students had been talking all this time about a course one of them had attended, run by a Buddhist monk and which was about the importance of being fully present and aware!

One cannot enter the Matrix carrying a bag full of personal programmes and preconceptions and expect to be aware of what is actually present.

Unless you are a Holy man/woman/guru - without the pressures of daily life such as paying the bills and keeping a roof over your head to consider - being constantly present and aware is likely to be beyond us. However, we can choose to be fully present and aware when it is important to be so. This state of relaxed alertness enables us to perceive without judgement or 'contamination' in terms of our own preconceptions or the chattering of our mind so we are fully present with whoever we are with or wherever we are.

'I can see you only when I look at you with a certain care in which neither of these things [judgement or analysis] is involved.' Jiddu Krishnamurti

Some of those who have spoken with the Dalai Lama have said that they felt then as though they were the only people in the world. Having observed the Dalai Lama responding to questions from an audience, I have no doubt in my mind that he was fully present with each person he addressed his answers to, and they in turn were very much aware of this.

This level of attention creates the foundation for open and honest exchange between people. We know when someone is 'not with us' when we are speaking to them, or is paying lip service to what we are saying and just waiting to speak again. We may also be very aware of those that are fully engaged with us and listening to what we have to say, appreciating who we are and accepting our maps of the world without judgement.

Application of this high level of presence is limitless – with relationships, clients, meetings, in buildings, or when you are enjoying a meal or a glorious sunset.

Total involvement brings a quality to these relationships which is here and now, and has no price.

How do we develop being present and aware?

There are steps that we use in training to enable students to develop this presence. We also use 'Anchoring', an NLP technique which is beyond the scope of this book, to anchor the desired programme so that it can be triggered into use when the student requires it.

Here, however, are the basic steps we lead our students through to enable them to create for themselves an internal model of being Present and Aware.

The Steps to developing being Present and Aware

1) Be Present
2) Select the Field of Awareness
3) Adopt an 'old friend' state of mind and body language.
4) Simply be - without judgement or analysis
5) You are now present and aware.

Before you start

Close your eyes and think of an old friend who you feel completely comfortable and relaxed with - someone in whom you have complete trust and with whom it is enough to just to be with; speaking is not required. Note how you feel as you think of them and also how you feel as you imagine being together.

(It may be that it is a place, rather than a person that produces that feeling - it does not matter which creates the feeling as long as you can experience and remember it).

HOLD THAT FEELING

An exercise in being present - Stage 1

1) Move into a relaxed position.
2) Bring focus of mind to relaxing limbs.
3) Notice the sensations of your body as a disinterested observer.
4) Let the sensations arise and pass.
5) Let all sounds and sensations drift by without any analysis.
6) Listen to your breathing.
7) Observe the sounds and movements of your body as you breathe.

>   Are you hungry?
>   Are you thirsty?
>   Right at this moment in time, right NOW.
>   There is no fear.
>   There is no past.
>   There is only the present.

Selecting your field of Awareness - Stage 2

Your chosen field of awareness can be as wide or as narrow as you wish. In a one-to-one situation the field can be formed to contain just the two of you including the space between; it can also include the environment you share.

Extend your feeling of 'presence' to the outer edges of your field of awareness.

Imagine that you have heard a strange sound in the night. Your representational systems (hearing, seeing and feeling) are heightened and fine-tuned to gather as much information as possible as to the source of the sound.

Adopt an 'old friend' state of mind and body - Stage 3

Starting within, access the feeling of being with a trusted friend.

Being without judgment or analysis - Stage 4

If you are fully present, have selected your FOR and have accessed and adopted the 'old friend' feeling correctly, you may find that you are in a state of sustained, clear open-mindedness - an observer of events with no interest invested in the outcome.

How will you know you have achieved being Present and Aware - Stage 5?

You will be in a state of relaxed alertness with a feeling of inner peace. You may also experience a profound feeling of gratitude.

With a little practice the process from 1 to 5 will speed up, as your subconscious mind recognises what you are doing and moves you through the stages more quickly. In this state of mind your right brain now has a chance to provide you with creative insights in response to the situation you have before you.

Why have we left it until now to provide you with this exercise when we have already accessed and are involved with the Matrix?

Because if we had started with this exercise you would not have had the experience of recognising the involvement of your personal programming and how it gets in the way. Re-doing the earlier exercises now from a position of being Present and Aware will give you some personal insight into how the conscious mind gets in the way and how much more is available to us within and outside of the field when we clear a space in our minds. Your new experience will be a different one.

You have also created the conditions for insight and creativity to arise.

7

FOCUS

Unlocking the power of a focussed mind

Accessing the energy field of a friend several hundred miles away, Susanne asked me, 'How do I know if the emotions that I am feeling are not my own?'

My response was, 'Where is your attention focussed, on the other person or yourself?'

Receptors and Energetic Change

Having formed your Frame of Reference, your receptors pick up an energetic change, or a quality within the field that attracts your attention. Having brought your full attention to this point or area, depending on the type of signal you are receiving, you have choices to make. If what attracted your attention was an area in the process of change or has the potential for change, bringing your full attention and your focus to this area will accelerate the process of change.

Those of you who are working in the field of complementary medicine, do not take my word for it, try it for yourself!

Those who use receptors to identify energetic change in fields, including the medical profession, can use scanning to identify the source of energetic change, and focus to identify the location and depth of the source.

For energy workers transmission of the potential for energetic change may appear to be coming from the surface of the human body. Closer investigation, however, reveals that the transmitter is in fact deep inside the body. Change may be facilitated by focus, like a laser beam on the point of transmission.

Receiving Emotional Resonances

If you are seeking information through Emotional Resonances make sure that you are prepared for any response **before** you ask the question. You will hear the words and the answer but your focus must be on the 'transmitter', the person who is responding to your question and on the ER response. Is the spoken answer congruent with the transmitted emotional response?

Whatever your reason for your investigative questioning you now have a starting point to explore the reason(s) for the conflicting information.

Focus – what depth?

Doctors, body and energy workers working with energetic change may find when scanning their client that there is an active energetic transmission in evidence but that the source of that activity cannot be located.

For those working with energy systems such as meridians, it is time to think outside of the box. Move your focus through the skin and muscle into the major joints in the body, the shoulders and hips – quickly check these out and then, if needed, move on to other joints. Where do your receptors record a sharp increase in energetic activity?

If you have still not found the source of the energetic transmission it is time to carry out an MRI with your mind, bringing your focus to bear at different depths in the body, scanning different structures and organs. For identification, it really helps if you know the main components and layout of the human body.

Having found the source, ask which tool will facilitate the required energetic change. Focus on the source of the energetic transmission is one of the tools that can be used to access areas that are difficult to get to.

Sometimes an emotional resonance is transmitted with a big energetic change. If recognised and intercepted, what is the information that this ER conveys?

We will explore using focus in other situations later in this book.

8

FINGERPRINTING

Once the connection is made on an energetic level between two vibrating energetic bodies the connection is always there. If one field transmits, all connected fields receive whether they are aware of it or not.

Although we are a constantly changing, expanding and contracting mass of frequencies, within each of us is a recognisable, unchanging element. We call this unchanging element the 'Fingerprint'.

Imagine listening to a piece of music you know that you have not heard before but you are aware of something that is familiar to you and you are sure the composer is Beethoven. The piece of music subsequently turns out to have been written by Beethoven.

That recognisable and familiar aspect of each of us and everything else is the 'Fingerprint'.

Receiving transmissions

The 'mother and child' situation we related to earlier is a very good example of a distress signal being received (by the mother) from a familiar fingerprint (the child).

Once we realise that we are constantly receiving signals transmitted from a known source, identification of the 'transmitter' becomes easier. We may now also become aware that many of the fleeting thoughts and emotions we experience are not of our own making. With practice we filter out all but the strong signals and move through our database of well-known fingerprints to identify the source of the transmission. Usually, however, when the signal is received, the transmitter is immediately identified if it is from a loved one or from close family or friends.

I was finishing my coffee and was preparing to go out for the day when I suddenly became overwhelmed with strong feelings of dizziness, nausea and complete disorientation. My Aunt Rita in a care home on the Isle of Bute came immediately to mind. I picked up the phone and called the care home.

'How is my aunt today?' I asked the care-worker who answered the phone.

There was a slight pause, and then she answered, 'She's fine, why do you ask?'

'No real reason,' I lied, 'I just wondered how she was.' End of conversation!

Two weeks later I visited my Aunt in Bute. Walking through the main door of the house, I was seized by one of the care-workers whose first words were:

'You scared the s**t out of us when you called. When the phone rang your aunt had just had some sort of seizure and we were rushing to attend to her.'

It was the first day of the Remote Viewing workshop and Stella and I were preparing to assist the teacher who had come all the way from Nevada, USA.

Ready to start the workshop, I became aware of my own increasing anxiety, and had begun to wring my hands which were bathed in sweat. My face had apparently gone white. I realised that this anxiety was not 'mine' but, having scanned friends and family, I had no idea of the source of the transmission. After about an hour I started to recover and eventually was able to start assisting in the workshop.

Two weeks later I went to visit a disabled client ('D') who lived in a special home. D had a number of disabilities; he had learning difficulties; he had physical disabilities; he was also epileptic. Sitting next to D, I suddenly recognised something. Within our frame of reference, I was aware of D's fingerprint, which was familiar although I had not made any attempt to access and remember it.

I took his carer to one side and asked her if anything had happened to D at exactly two weeks to the day at 10 am. The care-worker pulled out the book to look and see if anything had been noted there. Then she remembered. At around 10 am on that day, D had had a grand mal seizure and, as she put it, 'went down like a giant Redwood'. On coming round it seems he was very upset and anxious but after about an hour had returned to normal.

Here are two examples of strongly transmitted signals overriding filters and being received by an aware receiver. In the first case of my aunt, her fingerprint was well known to me, so the transmission was received and the transmitter was quickly and easily identified. In the case of D, I had neither consciously looked for nor identified his fingerprint at any time, but I was very much aware of our frame of reference when we were together. Thus the connection was made between D and me, although I was largely unconscious of it. Again, the transmission was sent and received, even though at the time I could not identify the source of the transmission.

It would appear that once the connection is made on an energetic level between two vibrating energetic bodies the connection is always there. If one transmits, all connected fields receive, whether they are aware of it or not.

Mostly we dismiss the momentary fluctuations in feelings and thoughts. This is similar to someone unknowingly sending out a cry for help through a mass mail-out to all known email addresses. It may come to our notice, or we receive the transmission and our filters put it into the junk mail box.

Scanning for a known Fingerprint

One can also scan for a fingerprint and access the energetic and emotional conditions of that person.

If Stella or I travel alone, we can keep in contact and assured of the traveler's well-being by accessing their fingerprint and checking for emotional resonances. Thus assured, we can relax in the knowledge that all is well. [1]

In this case, I am not in the car with Stella and she is not with me in our home. We are in a 'place' but not a physical location. We are with each other in another dimension, a temporary locality. If Stella is driving she may or may not be aware that I am with her, or more accurately, that **we are together in a 'non-locality' in the Energetic Matrix**.

Distance is no barrier to creating change.

So, we can receive energetic and emotional signals from an identifiable transmitting source and even strong ones which override our filters from a source we may not be able to identify. In some cases it may just be that our receivers are sensitive to certain transmissions from an unknown source. We can scan our database of known fingerprints, make a connection in real time and access the energetic and emotional situation there.

Once locked into the fingerprint and having accessed the energetic condition, we can create changes by identifying and focussing strongly on the active areas/points until the change takes place and the activity calms down. (Other ways of creating energetic changes over distance are mentioned in a later chapter.)

Open up for any emotional resonances that may be in evidence on your 'arrival', be open to emotional changes as you work within the energetic field.

As a general rule, only access another person's fingerprint by invitation of the person, or perhaps a relative if the person is not in a position to make their own decisions.

The Alert Team

Developing the ability to access an unknown fingerprint and create change is included in the 3rd two day module of our basic training in Waveform. Amongst our Waveform graduates are volunteers who have become highly skilled in fingerprinting, accessing information and creating change over any distance.

These volunteers access fingerprints that are unknown, create changes in the individual's energetic field and pass back information on what they have found, the energetic changes made and any emotional information to ourselves for the client.

We receive requests for assistance from all over the world, most of which are from people we do not know. The requests for help are for conditions that range from accidents to injuries of all kinds as well as terminal illness.

'Fingerprinters' work independently of each other, and if they arrive 'on site' and find nothing to do they exit the site. Usually this means that one of their colleagues has recently accessed the client and created changes where it was required. Sometimes one fingerprinter accessing the client's fingerprint recognises the presence of one of their colleagues already with the client.

Accessing an unknown fingerprint

How can a fingerprinter access an unknown fingerprint?

There is always a connected chain of links to one of us from the client or whoever asked for our help on their behalf. I act as a 'beacon' from which the fingerprinter locates the fingerprint of the client, as I have already made a connection with the client through the enquirer. The fingerprinter knows my fingerprint, and locates the client through me by accessing and tracing the unknown connection within my field. It is much easier and faster to do than it is to explain the process. A photograph of the client makes it very easy for the alert team to contact them.

Fingerprints - Once Connected, always Connected!

Once the connection is made on an energetic level between two vibrating energetic bodies the connection is always there. If one transmits all connected fields receive, whether they are aware of it or not. Those that have connected with a fingerprint which is known or unknown will always be able to make that connection, no matter where the person is or how long a time has passed since they were last in contact.

When we become aware of being able to detect individual fingerprints, the past and the future become open and accessible in a way that one would not have considered possible. We now have opportunities to resolve issues that have affected our lives and which we have carried with us, perhaps for decades.

[1]We do this from choice and with each other's knowledge and consent. In *most other circumstances without consent this would be an unacceptable invasion of privacy.'*

9

FREQUENCIES AND THE
HUMAN ENERGY FIELD

'Good Vibes, Man!'

Each of us is a mass of changing frequencies - we expand, contract and transform. Transformation creates a change in the whole energetic system. For healers and energy workers transformation in the energetic system is the first step towards self-healing. Transformation also stimulates changes in the HEF which create a new Frame of Reference.

I had always suspected that frequencies were somehow a major part of the workings of the human energy field and the healing processes of the body. It is really easy to say that the HEF is a 'mass of changing frequencies'. Proving this to yourself is difficult enough without having to prove it to someone else.

In the year 2000 an experiment took place in Glasgow which confirmed this belief and expanded our view of the nature and workings of the human energy field. The experiment was set up using a frequency generator, the receptor skills of our early Waveform graduates and a number of willing volunteers.

Amongst our many realisations from this experiment was that, using our receptors, we could identify individual frequencies that appeared to be on the point of change. This change can be likened to a piece of music at the point of changing key and moving into another mood at a different pace.

Using our minds we were able to create the conditions for change to take place. We also learned that changes could take place very quickly once the active frequency was identified and this was often followed by an emotional resonance.

We also realised that frequencies could be identified and changed over any distance, and this has proved to be very useful for our 'Alert' group. Time is also not an obstacle to using frequencies. Frequencies are a very useful tool when you are using timelines to access events in the past which have had debilitating repercussions over many years such as headaches and IBS.

Frequencies are also very useful in situations where 'hands on' treatments are either inappropriate or unacceptable.

We have barely touched on the amazing story of frequencies and how much they are a part of our lives. Our experience is, however, that the energetic structure of the HEF responds to and works within natural laws already known to science.

Frequencies as a tool are yet another example of the amazing power of our minds.

10

PERSONAL ALIGNMENT

In order to change the world we have first to
change ourselves – and then just be us!

Each of us in our own way strives to be happy, whatever the word 'happy' means to us. On those rare occasions when someone actually asks us what would make us happy, we are often stuck for a reply. Replies, when we are able to provide them, are often couched in terms of what we 'don't want'. We don't want to be poor/stuck in this dead end job etc. That there is no clear vision of a future of what we really want is often down to conflict within ourselves, parts of us that are not working in unison for our common good.

Personal Alignment is the bringing together in agreement of our head and our heart, the conscious part of ourselves, and the subconscious part of ourselves.

Unity of head and heart brings us more in contact with the Universe, to which we are already connected through the subconscious mind.

The Universal wisdom of the subconscious mind.

Each person has some idea of the parts of their lives that are not working for them as they would like. Being attuned to the subconscious mind as well as the conscious mind provides insight as to how we are managing our lives. We are often deaf to an internal voice that is providing us with wisdom from the depths of our being. This voice also holds the key to our internal programming built upon our experiences from birth to the present time, much of which is out of date, no longer serves us and creates limiting beliefs which damage our self-esteem.

We have within us the means to make the changes that will serve us in the manner that we would wish. These are choices **we** make and are not imposed upon us by others with their own individual 'maps of the world'. We can start by being more aware of how we respond emotionally to events in our lives - that is becoming more in tune with our subconscious.

We are already aware that our conscious mind and subconscious mind are not always in agreement[1]. When we align the conscious and subconscious minds, decision making is based on what will make us happy, what feels good, taking into consideration the changes that will have to take place.

For example, if what will make you happy is moving to the Mediterranean and living in a hut by a beach, changes that take place will include moving from where you live at the moment, who you might be living with and what will you do to earn a living. What will you have to give up to make the move? How will you earn the money to just live, day by day? Does what you will gain by making the move outweigh what you will lose?

Alignment does not throw out the practicalities of such a decision taking place but includes and recognises as being very important how we feel about our choice, particularly if the decision is a life-changing one. We also have the opportunity to address the fears that arise from such a decision e.g. our old programming - is it relevant?

When we choose self-alignment we connect to the part of us that the Universe listens to and acts upon - the heart.

If a client cancels or postpones an appointment my wife always asks me, 'Why did you do that?'

She is absolutely right of course, I did cancel the client!

My head says 'I need the cash', and my heart says, 'It is a beautiful day and I really want to be out in the woods by the stream, or on the Loch in my Kayak'.

The Universe listens to the heart not the head.

Message transmitted loud and clear – message received and acted upon.

How many times has something similar happened to you?

If your head and heart are in conflict over something start a discussion. In the case of my cancelled client this is what I could have done if I had realised at the time I was sending out a clear message of cancellation. (I know better now!)

Take the disagreement outside of yourself.

Select two objects, say an apple and a banana (anything will do) and have one in your left hand and one in your right hand. Decide which fruit is the head and which the heart.

Let the discussion begin – out loud!

Apple (Conscious mind)
'We needed the money to pay the bills.'

Banana (Subconscious Mind)
'But you are saying that you want to go kayaking.'

Apple
'I realise that but we still need the cash to pay the bills. If we go kayaking we lose money.'

Banana
'I'm only doing what you asked me to do; what we really want is no client.'

Apple (Conscious mind)
'Ok, so what decision can we come to where we are both happy?'

Banana
'I don't care as long as we go kayaking!'

Apple
'The weather looks good, so we could see the client first, and go kayaking afterwards. It will still be light and there is no wind.'

Banana
'But what if the weather changes?'

Apple (Conscious Mind)
'We have no clients tomorrow. If the weather changes this afternoon we could go kayaking tomorrow morning. Is this a deal?'

Banana (Subconscious Mind)
'It's a deal! Shake on it!'

Head and heart are in agreement. They are congruent, client arrives on time. Head and heart go kayaking. Head and heart are now pulling together – inner conflict gone.

When having an inner debate - say between A and B - don't give in easily on either side. Put up the best argument for the case of both head and heart as each is doing its best for you. Represent each point of view as best as you can, only then will you be truly aligned with the outcome.

This was a simple example of bringing agreement and congruence to a not very serious situation. In serious and life changing situations the principles of discussion remain valid.

It is a good idea to address old, out-of-date and self-limiting programmes which hold you back and get in the way of the progress of alignment. The more old programmes that you clear out or update the more you will appreciate who you really are, what you are capable of and what you want in life. This realisation brings with it a lightness and clarity that was not there before.

Regarding programming, I suggest that you do not try and change everything at once but take one thing at a time. There may be a domino effect from one major resolution which may remove other limiting programmes. However, others may appear that you were not aware of. Take it easy and take things at your own pace.

The most effective way of addressing out-of-date programmes and limiting beliefs is by personal one-to-one coaching. Unfortunately we are not able to go more deeply into methods of addressing out-of-date programmes in this book.

In our workshops we enable our students to connect to their subconscious mind. What they decide to change in themselves is entirely their choice. We only provide the method and assistance as requested.

When our out-of-date programming is being addressed and head and heart are aligned, we no longer have internal conflict without knowing 'why or what it is', but we now also have a means to address this. We move forward in confidence, knowing clearly that this is what we want. This does not mean that there is no longer any incongruence, only that it is immediately recognised and dealt with.

The Universe has always listened to us and we are now listening to the Universe.

[1](Chapter - Emotional Resonances - Question and answer – Is there congruence between the conscious and unconscious mind?)

11

ENERGY AND SPIRIT

'If you can only rid yourself of conceptual thought, you will have accomplished everything. Discuss it as you may, how can you even hope to approach the truth through words? Those who seek the truth by means of intellect and learning only get further and further away from it. Not till your thoughts cease all their branching here and there, not till you abandon all thoughts of seeking for something, not till your mind is motionless will you be on the right road to the Gate.'

We have now come full circle because the simple rules about entering the Energetic Matrix are the same rules that open the doors to enlightenment, whatever that may mean to you.

However, awareness of energy and the ability to voyage through the Energetic Matrix are not the same as the realisation of one's Spirituality and oneness with the Universe. Expanding awareness opens the door to the Energetic Matrix and also the Universal Mind.

Here we are faced with a challenge. Direct experience of energy, and the knowledge that it has no borders in time and space, raises questions about us as individuals, and our place in the Universe.

The music of the Universe

If you want to know what your place is in the Universe - how you fit in - just listen to a piece of music being played by a large orchestra.

You are a part of the universal orchestra, playing a universal piece of music. That piece of music has been playing since the beginning of time. Like a symphony it has different movements, progressing from one to the other, there are changes of key, mood and tempo but the orchestra remains the same. You are a part of that universal orchestra, adding to its depth and colour. As long as you listen to the music you will contribute to the quality of sound, the magnificence of the composition and you will recognise your place within the universal orchestra. You are both the orchestra and the music.

The minute that you cease to listen to the music you will be 'out of time' with the rest of the orchestra. The moment that you realise that you are, for example, a 'flute', and then focus on just being a flute, listening to the flute and the flute's part in the symphony without listening to the rest of the orchestra, the music continues without you and you become separate from the universal symphony.

Be a flute, but listen to the universal music in order to play your part in the wholeness of the universal orchestra. The universal music is then an expression of you and you are an expression of the universal music.

Not above, not separate but **integrated**.

That said, it does not mean that you cannot lead a human life, living and loving on a day to day basis. This universal music is part of life as we know it as human beings. Heaven and earth are not separate places; they co-exist and it is the realisation of this wholeness that makes us complete human and also spiritual beings.

Moving with the music brings wholeness, joy, belonging and your perception of 'ordinary' life changes.

The trees in the woods, that you are used to walking through, welcome you.

The wind moving the branches of the trees is now seen as a dance to which you are invited.

You are with friends. You smile and feel deep gratitude in your heart.

12

DISTANCE AND TIME - PAST, PRESENT AND FUTURE

'Is what we see now as the present a re-treading of the past from a future no longer remembered?'

Past, present and future are fully present - you have only to change how you look in order to see they are there.

The relationship between the past, the present and the future was once described to me like this:

Imagine you are travelling in a train. Looking out through the window you see the countryside passing by sequentially, moving steadily in one direction. Now imagine you are standing on top of the train. You can see where you have been, where you are and also where you are going even though you have not arrived there yet.

Past, present and future are fully present. You have only to change how you look in order to see they are there.

The past is not lost - all that has ever happened can be accessed.

As a trained Remote Viewer, I do not need any further evidence that the past is accessible now in real time and can be experienced by all our senses. Many memories are stimulated by a trigger of some kind - a piece of music, the smell of a flower or of perfume, an object seen, an emotion felt, a sunset.

Some of these memories are kept alive by trauma that was experienced at that time, others because remembering them makes us feel good, such as sharing a sunset in the arms of the person we love, or a delicious smell reminding us of the food vendors on the streets of Hong Kong on a warm evening with friends.

It would appear that not only is nothing lost that has taken place in the past, but we can still access an event in real time and we can also uncover information that we may have not been aware of, or which was not even available to us at that time.

We know very little about what our minds are capable of and it is easy to challenge anyone who says that if something cannot be proved it doesn't exist. Ask the question, "Prove to me that memory exists". Memory is used constantly in our daily lives, and whilst we have an idea of **how** memories are stored, we do not have a precise location for **where** any memory is stored.

We can have full sensory awareness of all our memories.

Using the right 'triggers', long-forgotten memories can be recalled and accessed, for example memories that reveal events that may have led to migraine head-aches in later life. If we make ourselves open to energetic change and emotional resonances, time can be rewound to the source of the headache and which can then be treated energetically in real time.

For many if not all of us there are issues, memories of unresolved situations, those 'What was that all about?' moments. Some are just unresolved puzzles, others are serious enough to stick in our minds; the hurt, the outrage, the anger and confusion are carried forward, affecting our lives and our relationships.

We can access these long past situations and can use our energetic awareness to reveal information that was not available to us at the time. We can gain answers to questions, access the feelings of those present to gain an understanding of what lay behind the words and the actions at that time. Information that was there all the time but not accessible to you is now revealed.

What you have realised and learned will not change the events that took place, but having access to this previously unknown information may bring a measure of understanding and closure. The ending of your chosen event may not be a happy one but you have a chance to know all there is to know about what happened. For many people clarity brings closure and release from the bonds of the event. With situations that include abuse, there are other measures that need to be taken to release the bonds of the trauma and bring freedom for the person involved.

13

HUMOUR AND THE
ENERGETIC/SPIRITUAL PATH

'The creative process flourishes when accompanied with a sense of humour. Humour increases the potential for divergent thinking and the ability to solve complex problems. By linking previously unconnected areas of the brain, humour forges new associations involving existing concepts.'

Although many profound personal realisations have come about as a result of personal trauma, this does not have to be the only driver for personal and profound energetic and spiritual realisation. One does not have to approach training as though one is attending a funeral - your own funeral. The journey is exciting, and there are many magical places to explore and enjoy.

Humour transcends the intellect, which may comprehend what the joke is about but it is the right brain - the creative side - which enjoys the meaning of the joke, without necessarily being able to explain why it is funny. When a joke has to be explained the funniness is lost.

Zen Buddhism is known for its often bizarre humour and it has a purpose. Behind the humour is a message which bypasses the intellect. If you can intuitively understand the message hidden within the humour then you've cracked it - you have the combination to the Universal Safe.

Some years ago when the Dalai Lama was in the UK, I watched a programme about him on television. He was eating food at a table and was chuckling away whilst listening to a radio which was beside him. I wondered what he felt was so funny and I then realised that a newsreader on the radio had said, '..and the police continued their high speed car chase through the streets of Birmingham at 30 miles per hour!'

The point I am getting to is, be easy on yourself, relax and enjoy the journey – have fun and you enhance the conditions that enable creativity and self-realisation. Both are products of the right brain.

Humour breaks down barriers between people and also the barriers we construct within ourselves, including perhaps the status in which we believe others should regard us. These are all barriers, preconceptions about who we think we are.

Humour enables us to let down some of these barriers, taking off the pressure we impose upon ourselves – creating a space for growth, creativity and intuition to arise.

In the fantasy film 'Willow', a baby is found floating on a raft on the river that flows past the village of Hobbit like people called Nelwyns, and a deputation led by the baby's finder, Willow Ufgood, is about to leave their village in the woods to return the baby to its own race of people, the Daikini.

The High Aldwin, the Nelwyns' village Sorcerer, addresses the deputation before it starts its Journey.

The outer world is no place for a Nelwyn. Give the baby to the first Daikin you see and then hurry home.'

He stoops and picks up an apple from the ground, utters some magic words and throws the apple into the air, where it turns into a bird.

High Aldwyn: 'Go in the direction the bird is flying!'

Burgelcutt: 'He's going back to the village!'
High Aldwyn: 'Ignore the bird. Follow the river!'

Although the film is complete fiction, this little episode is a wonderful example of status and power poking fun at itself. The scene could also have another message. Keep things simple! This scene I remember with fondness and is a favourite clip on YouTube. To get the full impact of the scene it has to be seen and heard. Better still, see the film, the words alone do not do it justice.

The route that you choose to take on your own personal path is up to you so check all routes with your subconscious mind and see what you feel happy with. The chances are that this is the route from which you will derive the most benefit. As you will eventually discover, the energy field has its own sense of humour. I hope that you are ready to enjoy the joke and laugh aloud.

14

Summary

'All that we are is the result of what we have thought; it is founded on our thoughts, it is made up of our thoughts. If a man speaks or acts with an evil thought, pain follows him, as the wheel follows the foot of the ox that draws the carriage.

All that we are is the result of what we have thought; it is founded on our thoughts. If a man speaks or acts with a pure thought, happiness follows him like a shadow that never leaves him.'

The Journey

Our journey started with recognising the **energetic environment** and experiencing the many textures and qualities that are the most tangible to us. Addressing **preconceptions and personal programming** is for many the most commonly recurring challenge encountered throughout the voyage.

The tools of **receptors and emotional resonances** demonstrate that the **Energetic Matrix** is 'active' and responds to us. These tools also demonstrate that we are constantly transmitting energetic and emotional information which is accessible to everyone. These tools enable us to connect to and communicate with Universal Energy.

Being present and aware enables us to receive all information, energetic and emotional, within our chosen **frame of reference,** whilst allowing strong transmissions from outside of the **Frame of Reference** to also be received. **Being present and aware** enables us to receive information in a clear non-judgemental way. In this way we perceive the reality of what is there, instead of colouring the truth with our programming, prejudices, preconceptions and map of the world.

The **Energetic Matrix** is not hampered by limitations of the physical, therefore we can 'be' wherever we wish. **Fingerprinting** creates a focus for us. A **fingerprint** is constantly transmitting like a beacon; all we have to do is to locate and travel down the beam.

Our skills of **receptors** and **emotional resonances** are unhampered by distance or time and **focus** enables us to be effective wherever we are, whether physically present with the source of the transmission or in a **non-locality**.

The accessibility of time means that we can address the source of our limiting beliefs and our out-of-date programming - updating our internal 'software' and letting go of what is no longer serving us.

Alignment between the conscious and subconscious minds brings us in contact with the source of our existence – the Universal Mind.

We now have **congruence** in our decision making and expectations in life. We are now also fully aware of the messages we send out and which are acted upon by the Universe.

The power of your thoughts

Our experiences to date have enabled us to move easily from what might be considered normal life into the **Energetic Matrix** where the rules of 'normal life' do not apply. Our mind is free to roam and within the **Matrix** it has enormous power to influence our ordinary lives. Distance and time have a completely different meaning - both are fluid and ever present.

You have abilities beyond imagination. Becoming aware of what you are capable of is like waking up from a deep sleep. You also have great responsibility to yourself and to others.

Actions and thoughts in the Matrix have repercussions in the physical and emotional levels of ordinary life.

Once these words have been fully understood and truly experienced, the words 'You reap what you sow' take on a whole new meaning. All thoughts 'positive' and 'negative' towards others have immediate personal consequences for you.

When you fully realise that your thoughts immediately form an equally powerful reality in you, you will consider carefully how you choose to feel. You are no longer protected from the results of your thoughts by your internal **filters** or lack of connection with your subconscious mind. You can no longer say 'I did not know'.

You now realise that you are a reflection of what you put out to the Universe. This realisation carries with it a great deal of responsibility. It also creates for you an opportunity to feel love, caring, joy, confidence and happiness in your life, purely by wishing it for others.

The path toward this realisation is your own path.

The path and the destination are right here, within you.

The time is **now**.

To Boldly Go....

Perhaps reaching the end of this book you are now ready to start your journey.

It may be that you have already been on a path, but was it **your** path you were walking? This book was written for you, so remove all your labels and concepts, challenge your programming as it arises and your logic which tries to deny you the reality of your direct experience. Walk your own path.

Put down the books that narrow your focus and turn your back on any teaching that places limitations on your abilities and forward movement in life.

Finally, put this book aside and step through the gate into the **Self-Aware Universe**.

Enjoy the Voyage – it is called LIFE!

REFERENCES

1) William Shakespeare – Romeo and Juliet

2/3/4/5/7/8/ M.Webster - Waveform.

6) Blake, William. *The Pickering Manuscript. The William Blake Archive*. Ed. Morris Eaves, Robert N. Essick, and Joseph Viscomi. December 2011. Web. Accessed 19 July 014. <http://www.blakearchive.org/>." Stuart Holroyd - Krishnamurti – The man the Mystery and the Message

9) 1960s New Age Saying

10) MW Inspired by Stuart Hepburn

11) John Blofeld –'The Zen Teaching of Huang Po on the Transmission of Mind'. The Buddhist Society

12) M.Webster – 'Bi-location – Somewhere in Time'.
   http://www.human-memory.net/processes_storage.html

13) Information Age Education – Oregon USA.
   Willow. Fantasy film by George Lucas, directed by Ron Howard.

14) The Dhammapada (Words of the Buddha)

TRAINING IN WAVEFORM

Waveform is a process that enables the student to learn about the Energetic Matrix through direct experience. Waveform allows students to recognise the natural tools that they already have with which they can access the Matrix. Students are then shown how these skills and their experiences in the Matrix can greatly enhance the quality of their everyday life and work.

Basic Training is in 3 x 2 days modules. Post-Graduate training is provided through 'Pathfinder' workshops which further develop students' energetic skills and take them deeper into the Energetic Matrix.

Training is in a relaxed atmosphere with humour and a low student to trainer ratio.

For more information please see www.waveformenergetics.com

Contact

For information regarding training in the following countries please contact Mike and Stella Webster - mike@waveformenergetics.com.

Australia, Austria, Canada, France, Germany, New Zealand, Switzerland and United Kingdom.

AUTHOR'S
BIOGRAPHICAL DETAILS

Mike Webster is the founder of Waveform Energetics, one of the world's most advanced energy awareness, training and research organizations, with graduates and students from all walks of life in 10 different countries. Mike is also a Certificated NLP Master Practitioner and a professional Remote Viewer and Teacher. NLP and some aspects of Remote Viewing are incorporated in Waveform training.

Mike's first experience of the Energetic Matrix took place when he was only six years old and, after a spiritual experience at the age of 26, he became interested in Buddhism.

Whilst farming in the Orkneys in the early 1980s, Mike became apprenticed to a unique spiritual training group. The training he received completely changed the course of his life. Nine years later, Mike had a profound realisation which became known as 'Waveform'.

With this experience came the realisation that the 'key' that opens the door to the secrets of the universe was 'readiness'. Waveform is a means of developing this 'readiness' which opens the door to the secrets of the Universe.

Mike has been a columnist for a Complementary Health Magazine and publishes articles on Complementary Medicine, health, energy, and the path of spirituality in a number of periodicals. He is also an invited speaker at seminars and conferences on the subject of energy and spirituality and how they can empower each of us in our ordinary lives.

Mike and his wife Stella live beside Loch Lomond in Scotland. They provide coaching and consultations for individuals, businesses and teams in growth and development, and provide workshops in the unique process of Waveform across the world.

Printed in Great Britain
by Amazon.co.uk, Ltd.,
Marston Gate.